Praise for Love Poe

"These poems are a rem(
pause and return to the ever-unfolding wonder of the living
Earth."
—Micah Mortali, author of *Rewilding*

"This groundbreaking book opens new vistas of possibilities
for our relationship with nature. The poems and practices are
simple yet magical, lighting the way to a deeper connection."
—Joseph Bharat Cornell, author of *Sharing Nature* and
Flow Learning

"Kai's poems awaken my love of nature and life itself, like a
splash of spring rain and unfurling ferns renewing my heart
and soul. She awakens all the emotions—joy and sorrow,
delight and longing—and evokes a beautiful celebration of
the miracle of life on our amazing planet. When I enter these
pages it's as if I am at her side, and I feel deeply alive again."
—Rev. Connie L. Habash, MA, LMFT, author of *Awakening
from Anxiety*

"Kai's poetry is a gift from her heart to ours. This book is a
treasure chest of reverence, wisdom, playfulness, and
sacredness that embraces the mystery and reveals the
extraordinary within the ordinary. Take your time to read,
savor, and live this offering and feel the sacredness of it all."
—Bob Stahl, co-author of five books on mindful living,
including: *A Mindfulness-Based Stress Reduction Workbook,
Living With Your Heart Wide Open,* and *Calming the Rush of Panic*

"This collection offers a voice from the heart of the Earth to
us, and encourages us to offer our own voice of love to the
living beings who share our home places. This spirit of
interconnection with the natural world shines from each
page. Kai's poems also inspire us to recognize and honor the
poet within ourselves."
—Victoria Loorz, author of *Church of the Wild*

Love Poems from the Earth

An Invitation to an Intimate Connection with Nature

Kai Siedenburg

Illustrations by Mária Kersey

Our Nature Connection

Published by Our Nature Connection

 Our Nature Connection

To contact the author about booking workshops or ordering books in bulk, visit OurNatureConnection.com.

Cover design by Jeremy Thornton

Cover image by Kazutoki

ISBN: 979-8-218-11864-8

Library of Congress Control Number: 2022923907

Printed in the United States of America

OurNatureConnection.com

LovePoemsfromtheEarth.com

For all my relations,
and for the benefit
of all beings

The poems say,
shhhh.

The poems say,
listen.

The poems say,
we are everywhere...

if you listen deeply,
we will come to you.

The poems say,
we are here.

CONTENTS

INTRODUCTION

A few years ago, I had an experience with a tree that forever changed how I think about love. I was out for a solo hike in one of my favorite nature spots, a lushly wooded valley up the coast from my home in Santa Cruz, California. It was late afternoon, and most other hikers had already headed back, leaving me free to immerse myself in the forest and listen without distraction.

I was resting in the arms of a special tree friend, a majestic California bay laurel, reclining on a broad branch and gazing up into the graceful crown of the tree. The sun was low in the sky, and just a few branches near the top were still illuminated, swaying gently in the breeze.

I hadn't planned to stay long, since I wanted to hike out before dark, yet I sensed a clear invitation to linger that seemed to come directly from the tree. And when a tree speaks to me, I listen!

So, I nestled into the embrace of the bay tree and listened with my whole body. It was an experience I will always remember. I felt held and supported by much more than the strong branches holding me aloft, as though I was energetically merging with the tree. I sensed a level of unconditional love and acceptance I had never known before. It was one of the most powerful experiences of communion with another being in my life.

As I rested in the branches, a direct and powerful message came to me. It didn't just pop into my head. It emanated directly from the tree, from a source of living wisdom much greater than my own mind. I felt it permeate my body and soul with a profound sense of intuitive knowing.

The message was: *You can go to the natural world to help meet your needs for intimacy and connection and teach others how to do this.*

I knew in every fiber of my being that I had received a beautiful and sacred gift that would serve me for many years to come. I basked in this experience of love and communion. Unable to pull myself away, I stayed with my bay laurel friend almost until sunset and made it back to the trailhead just before dark. The hike out was peaceful and magical. I watched the light fade into rosy hues and then deeper shades of blue as the first stars pierced the darkening sky. Great horned owls hooted in the distance and the gentle chorus of crickets, tree frogs, and the murmuring creek brought a smile to my face. While I saw no other humans, I felt profoundly connected and anything but alone.

This moment was one of many turning points in a rich and fascinating journey that has transformed how I think about friends, family, and love, and how I meet my needs for connection—all for the better.

Looking for Love

Most of us are taught to look for love in certain places: in groups of like-minded people, at bars and parties, in carefully crafted profiles on glowing screens. We are not taught to look for it in the strong branches of trees, the delicate petals of flowers, or water gliding over stones. We are also trained to search for love primarily in the form of one idealized romantic partner, which limits our options and leaves many people lonely and longing for more connection.

What if we could snap out of the hypnotic trance of fairy tale romance and inhabit a wider, wilder, and more inclusive love story? One that enables us to escape from the cramped confines of the humans-only club and rewild our friendships and love lives—not to replace our human relationships, but to expand our circle of kinship? What if we knew that every being could be our friend and teacher, and that we can cultivate loving connections with trees, lakes, and special places in nature and experience the unconditional love we yearn for?

We would feel more love, and more loved. We would feel less alone and more connected. We would have a solid base of support we could count on in good times and bad—perhaps more than we can rely on some of our closest human relations. Our love lives would become broader, deeper, richer, and (yes) wilder!

While making friends with plants, birds, or creeks might sound strange to modern ears, it's healthy for us to experience profound love for nature and close friendships

4

with more-than-human beings. For most of our history on planet Earth, we lived in cultures that recognized all beings as our relations and revered the wisdom of nature. This innate love and kinship are still inside us, ready to be rekindled.

What do you look for in a friend? Someone who makes you smile? Who you feel comfortable with? Who lifts your spirits? Who accepts you exactly as you are? All this and more can be found in the natural world, where many forms and flavors of friendship can flourish...

The comfortable familiarity of a trail we have walked dozens of times and that reliably leaves us feeling calmer and happier. The everyday intimacy of tending a garden and helping plants grow. The safety of a forest glade that offers refuge when we are recovering from a painful experience. The palpable sense of support when we lean into a tree or lie down on the Earth, let the tears flow, and release our burdens. The unconditional love we share with our four-legged friends, who may provide our most steadfast source of companionship.

Nature can be viewed as a diverse and loving extended family that is always available to support us. It reminds us that we are part of a vast and beautiful web of life. It encourages our interests, draws out our strengths, and teaches us about what matters, like a healthy extended human family would. If we attune to it, the natural world can speak to us very deeply. As Indigenous people have known for millennia, all aspects of nature have wisdom and medicine to share, and respectful contact with nature allows us to access that medicine.

I'm not suggesting that everyone should abandon their spouses and families, head for the hills and look for love only outside the human world. I am suggesting that many of us could find love and connection more easily and happily by expanding our circle of kinship to include the natural world. Time and again, in both my personal practice and work with clients, I have seen how healing occurs when we shift from viewing nature beings as objects to approaching them as friends, relations, and allies.

5

Making friends with "other" beings and natural places is easier than you may think, and more like making friends with humans than you might expect. It starts with giving the spark of connection a chance—noticing who and what you feel instinctively drawn to and allowing those relationships to grow and blossom. A little time and attention can go a long way, especially when you are present and your heart is open. The practices chapter in this book can help light the path.

Of course, a friendship with a fern, a bluebird, or the ocean will be quite different from one with another human. You may need to go to them and meet on their terms. The connections will likely be less verbal and more visceral, embodied, and instinctual. Much of the communication will transpire at a level deeper than words.

Nature beings and places can be some of our most trustworthy and supportive friends. The quality of connection is often purer, simpler, and less fraught than human relationships. And contact with nature is so beneficial that it can nourish and heal us even at a distance, as when we visualize ourselves in a peaceful place outdoors or call on a nature ally to guide us during our day. We can even cultivate deep bonds with nature allies we never have physical contact with. For example, bison are among my allies, although I have only glimpsed them briefly and from a distance. Yet they responded to my request for an ally one day, and I have often felt their quiet strength when I needed it.

In these challenging times, it's easy to get overwhelmed and shut down. Yet it is more important than ever to keep our hearts and minds open to the natural world. Like wind-blown seeds, love sows more love. Whether for wild poppies along the roadside, the oak tree outside our window, or our four-legged companions, the more we feel and express love, the greater our capacity for love will be. Nourishing our innate love for nature inspires us to treat the Earth, her creatures, and each other with more care and respect, and is a surprisingly important key to restoring peace and balance in our lives and in the world. Put simply, loving this Earth is one of the most powerful things we can do for ourselves and our planet.

A Different Kind of Love Poem

So, this is a book of love poems—but not a "they kissed and then lived happily ever after" kind of love. These are a different kind of love poem, about a different kind of love... poems about the simple, elemental love of slivers of sunlight on a winter's day or a cool stream on a hot summer afternoon. Poems about the pure and primal love between a woman and a redwood, a woman and a river. Poems about the love of people for trees and (believe it or not) even the love of trees for people!

The title *Love Poems from the Earth* came through spontaneously while I was on silent retreat last fall, accompanied by a clear, embodied knowing that it was meant for my next book. You might ask, "Why not *Love Poems for the Earth*?" They are that too. But I wanted the title to emphasize that these poems are expressions of Earth's innate love and generosity. They are love poems *from* the Earth, co-created with beings and places in nature, infused with the wisdom of trees and birds, water and stone, and a testament to what becomes possible when we approach with respect and listen deeply. These are also love poems *for* the Earth, rooted in profound love and reverence for the natural world, and expressing affection, passion, and loving concern for the Earth and all beings.

"All creation is co-creation," writes systems architect Marcia Conner. So true! While I hold the pen and write the words, these poems are not mine alone. They are the work of many paws, wings, roots, and leaves, co-created through a process of deep and intentional listening. My experience is that the Universe (especially the more wild and natural corners of it) is brimming with creative energy and seeking human hosts to bring it into form.

Most of my poems emerge when I'm "alone" in nature or on silent retreat, and quiet inside and out. Stepping away from the relentless demands and distractions of modern life allows me to slow down, attune to the greater flow of creation, and receive its gifts. Typically, the poems come through effortlessly and organically. My task is to stay open and receive, not to direct the process. I see them as gifts from Earth and Spirit, medicine poems for my own healing and for others, meant to be shared.

Yet I have the privilege of being on retreat only a few days a year. So, how can I tap into creative inspiration the other 350-odd days? Over time, I have found many answers to that question. Regular time in nature with a focus on being quiet and receptive is essential. When I'm at home, it starts with protecting my space (by resisting impulses to check email or respond to external demands), then cultivating a peaceful and open state through prayer, visualization, energy medicine, or ceremony.

I have a regular place where I pray, at a large window where the morning sun streams in. I stand there like a tree and sense myself opening to the Earth below and the heavens above, or imagine a special redwood tree friend with me. Often I bring to mind some of the many gifts I've been given, say "thank you" a few times, or simply stand still and open myself to receive—any one of these will usually bring grateful tears.

Sometimes I call on my nature allies and ask for their guidance, or use a simple ceremony of walking away from the diversions of daily life and into a creative sanctuary where my guides surround me, nourishing my creativity and protecting me from distractions. I also draw on the power of sensory cues like the sound of a chime and the scent of sage from my garden to invoke a shift in state. Anything I do to calm my mind, ground my energy, and align with a larger flow of gratitude and guidance, even just for a minute, helps me be more creative.

Creating in this partnership with Earth and Spirit is a relatively recent development for me, an unexpected gift that came through when I started spending more solo time in nature 11 years ago. The introduction to the practices chapter shares more of this story, and the poems in the "Nature of Creation" section speak to the creative process.

I have almost no formal training in writing poetry. To this day, I don't know how to sit down and deliberately write a poem on a topic of my choosing. Even when I have a fervent desire to do so, the results are invariably awkward and unsatisfying for both me and the poem. Yet I *do* know how to invite the arrival of new poems, listen for those that are ready to be born, and walk hand in hand with them as they emerge in their own time.

While this is primarily a book of poetry, it also includes a chapter of nature practices. It is rare that you will find poems and practices commingling in one volume, but I encourage it because they offer direct pathways into deeper connection in distinct and complementary ways—and because I want to help you find pathways that work for you.

The poems evoke experiences of peace, beauty, and reverence, and speak directly to your heart and spirit. The practices offer simple ways to invite moments of peace, beauty, and reverence into your own life. Both extend gentle invitations into a world of authentic and nourishing connections with Earth and Spirit, ourselves and others.

I offer this book as an act of sacred service, with wholehearted respect for the wisdom of nature and deep gratitude for all my human and more-than-human teachers. May these poems and practices help you cultivate loving and respectful relationships with the natural world and live in harmony with yourself, other people, and all life!

ENCOUNTERS
WITH NATURE

Infused

When I
came here,

I was
an ordinary human,

full of
ordinary
human cares.

Now I am
infused
with blue of sky
and green of tree,

with song of bird
and hum of bee.

Although
my form
may appear
unchanged,

inside it's clear
I'm not
the same.

A Small Brush with Greatness

I had to wait
more than 50 years,
but it finally happened...

a wild bird
landed on me—

or more precisely,
on the edge
of my journal—

but since that journal
was on my lap,
and I had been
writing in it
for most of the morning,

it felt like
a part of me.

And when
the pine siskin
swooped down
from a nearby redwood,
landed on my journal,

and fixed me
with his
intense little gaze,

his bright black eyes
were only a foot away
from my brown ones.

So close!
So close!

Although
he was small in stature
(no more than five inches
from head to tail),

he was
a powerful presence,
a force of nature,

and I knew
in my bones
that I had
experienced
a brush with greatness.

Meeting with a Hawk Feather

The hawk feather
met me
just outside
my cabin,

as though
it had been
anticipating
my arrival.

It was right
on my path,
just a few feet
from the door,

with striking
dark brown
and white bands

that declared it
a red-shouldered hawk
tail feather.

Although
nearly weightless,
it was
a compelling presence.

Although lying still
on the Earth,
it might have been
soaring
through the sky
mere hours
or even moments ago.

Although silent,
it spoke to me
deeply.

I felt it say,

"You are
welcome here,

and you are free
to soar!"

Grumbling

I grumbled a little
when I was woken up
at 3:00 am
by a ruckus
outside my window—
a fox, as it turned out.

I grumbled a little more
when I was still awake
at 3:30, 4:00, and beyond,

and even more
when I woke up for good at 7:20,
feeling groggy due to
the interrupted sleep.

I grumbled about wanting
to be awake enough
to enjoy my last morning
in that special place.

Eventually
it dawned on me
that it was my grumbling
more than the lack of sleep
that was preventing me
from enjoying the morning,

that it was
a great privilege
to be near enough to a fox
to be woken up by her,

and that the experience
was not a rude awakening,

but rather a gracious invitation
to step outside
and share a magical moment
under a starry sky
with a rare and beautiful creature.

And so
I stopped
grumbling—

at least
about that!

April 6th

Today is April 6th.

My calendar says
"taxes."

Yet the call
of the wild
is too strong
to deny.

So I turn away
from the calendar,
walk out the door,

and transport myself
to a nearby state park,

where I
wander through
verdant green meadows,

behold
bumblebees blessing
lush fields of lupine,

share a quiet,
respectful encounter
with a handsome
gopher snake,

climb into
the branches
of a majestic oak tree,

and receive
several new poems

while nestled
in his branches.

At the time,
it seemed like
the most responsible
thing to do.

Would you
agree?

Thank You, Shoes

Most days,
I gratefully accept
the many gifts
my shoes give me—

keeping my feet
warm on a cold day,
cool on a hot day,
dry on a wet day;

shielding my skin
from thorns,
sharp stones,
bits of glass,
and so many
other things
I prefer not to tread on—

the everyday superpower
of being able to walk
on almost any surface
safely and comfortably.

But sometimes,
when the conditions
are right,

I love to
shed my shoes,

walk barefoot
on the Earth,

and feel
it all.

Barefoot Alchemy

The simple act
of removing
my shoes

transforms
an "ordinary" walk
in the woods

into a feast
of tantalizing
sensations,

an array of
irresistible
invitations,

a glorious reunion
between

the living
intelligence
of my feet

and the living
intelligence
of the Earth.

What My Feet Have Known

My feet,
unlike so many
of their modern kin,

have led
a rich
and adventuresome life,

with ample opportunity
to explore
the wonders
of the natural world.

They have known
the warmth
of sand
kissed by
a distant sun,

the freshness
of green grass
graced by
morning dew,

the smoothness
of stones
shaped by
millennia of
moving water.

They have been
intimately acquainted

with many streams
and many shores,

tasted exquisite
sensual delights,

and explored
extraordinary places.

They have known
what those
who spend
all their days
inside shoes
have forgotten.

A Good Amount

A good amount
of time
to go barefoot...

until I feel
like wearing shoes
again.

A good amount
of time
to be naked...

until I feel
like wearing clothes
again.

A good amount
of time
to stay outside...

until I feel
like going inside
again.

It can take
a good long time!

I Take Refuge

I take refuge

in the
quiet strength
of oaks,

the vibrant green
of new grasses,

the bright gold
of buttercups.

I take refuge

in the steady hum
of bees,

the gentle murmur
of streams,

the sweet songs
of sparrows.

I take refuge

in the warmth
of sun,

the freshness
of breeze,

the boundless blue
of sky.

I take refuge.

Just Outside My Window

Thank you,
wrens,

for gracing me
with your presence,

for blessing me
with your songs,

for reminding me
many times a day

that just outside
my window

are magical creatures
who sing and fly.

On the Eighth Day

And on the
eighth day,
I was bitten.

For seven days,
I immersed myself
in the wild
and peaceful woods.

For seven days,
I sat and walked
among
all manner
of intelligent life,

including
countless
winged insects.

Everywhere
I went,
they floated
in the air,
glinted
in the sun,

hummed
and chirped
among the
branches.

They landed on
my chair,
my clothes,
and my journal.

But save for
the occasional mosquito
in the evening,

not one
attempted
to bite me—
until the eighth day.

By the time
I felt the sting,
the venom
was already in—

a tiny yet potent
concoction
that would cause
my ear to redden,
swell, and itch
for several days.

I don't know
what motivated
the sting.

I chose
to regard it as a
pointed reminder
to listen—

and a small
price to pay

for eight days
of immersion
in the wisdom
and wonders
of nature.

Something Made Me

Something made me
look up from my journal
just in time

to glimpse
a bobcat
silently slipping
through the
dry creek bed—

a second later,
and I would have
missed her.

Something made me
go to a particular beach
just in time
to catch the thrilling sight
of dolphins leaping
from the water.

Something made me
alter my plans
and direction of travel
to go to another beach
on another day
just in time to see

the rare
and astounding sight
of humpback whales
mating near shore.

Something often makes me
begin a hike
on a mostly-rainy day

just in time
to get back
moments before
the next downpour.

Something often tells me to
include a certain something
in a group class,

and later
someone invariably tells me
how that particular piece
was exactly
what they needed.

So many times,

for reasons
that weren't
immediately apparent,

something has told me
to go to a certain place
at a certain time

or do things
in a certain way

that led to
moments of grace
I never could have predicted
or orchestrated.

What *is*
that something?

SEEING NATURE,
BEING NATURE

A Thousand Butterflies

Last night,
I dreamed

I had
a thousand butterflies
inside my heart,

rising
with a great joy
and lightness.

Effortlessly
they floated
into the vast blue sky,

and all about them
was a sense
of freedom
and celebration.

They were not
weighed down
by unnecessary burdens.

They were not bound
to anyone or anything
they did not love.

Last night,
I dreamed I had
a thousand butterflies

surrounding me
with soft wings
and bright colors.

I felt my burdens lift,
and I followed
their bright wings
to freedom.

Around Every Corner

Within
every seed

Beneath
every stone

Around
every corner

In every
quiet moment

so much
magic
and mystery

just waiting

to be
discovered.

Teach Us, Show Us the Way

Grains of sand,
gathering of tiny stones,
so solid yet so soft,

teach us,
show us the way.

Vast ocean,
ever-flowing and ever-changing,
touching many shores,

teach us,
show us the way.

Warm sun,
journeying through
immense darkness
to share your light,

teach us,
show us the way.

Cool breeze,
breath of ocean
and green leaves,

invisible
yet essential,

teach us,
show us the way.

*Poet's note: The title of this piece is borrowed from a poem
sometimes attributed to an anonymous Chinook author. However,
a leader of the Chinook Nation clarified that the author is
unknown and may not be of Chinook heritage.*

Too Beautiful

It's much too beautiful
to stay inside…

too beautiful
to let the ceiling
come between
me and the sky,

to let four walls
come between
my skin and the sun,

to let the floor
come between
my bare feet
and the living Earth.

On a day like this,
even a temple
can feel like a prison.

Late Bloomer

Compared to
most plants,
I am
a late bloomer.

It has
taken me
many years
to learn

what most
of them
master
in just
a few months—

to grow
and blossom
in the way
I am meant to...

and I am
still learning!

Red Tulips, Aging Gracefully

When I first met them,
I had no idea

the tulips
would express themselves
in entirely new ways
as they grew old—

no idea
the vibrant red
of their youth

would give way
to a more subtle
and varied
palette of colors—

muted carmine,
dusky violet,
soft gold.

I had no idea
they would age
so gracefully,

that their
"faded" glory
would be
more intriguing,
more alluring,

and indeed
more glorious

than their
bright and brassy youth.

The Poppies Put Their Heads Together

It's as though
the poppies
put their
silky orange
heads together
and said,

"People,
it's been
a rough year.

The world needs
us now.

So get
out there
and shine!

Bloom like
you've never
bloomed before!

Give it all
you've got!"

Spring Rapture

Spring!

I can hardly bear
to be indoors!

Every fiber
of my being
yearns to be out
among those who are
growing and blooming.

I am
under the influence
of flowers,

powerless
to resist
their charms—

and really,
what would be
the point

of attempting to
remain sober
in the face of
intoxication

that is
so natural
and beneficial
to the spirit?

The Winged Mind

Those who
claim to know

see swallows
swoop and dive
through the sky

and chalk it up
to a primitive
animal instinct
to find food.

But who are we
to know
the minds
of these
winged beings?

Who are we to say
their acrobatic flight
isn't partly
for sheer joy?

News of the World

I read
the news of the world
every day—

but not on
a glowing screen

or a gray page
of newsprint.

I read it in
bright green leaves
illuminated by
the morning sun,

clouds drifting
and dissolving
in the blue sky,

bees humming
among the blossoms,

the sweet songs
of sparrows,

the harsh call
of the red-tailed hawk.

I'm aware
that I don't
fully understand
the nuances
of each piece,

that I am
woefully ignorant

of the millennia of history
and the rich cultural context
behind each story.

Still, in my
fumbling human way,
I grasp
the basic gist
of what I see and hear,

and it is mostly
good news.

Pardon Me, Plants

Pardon me, plants,
for all the times
I've walked right by

without acknowledging
your existence,
let alone appreciating
your exquisite beauty,

for all the times
I've underestimated
your intelligence

or failed to respond
to attempts
at kind and respectful
communication.

Pardon me, plants,
for all the times
I have taken
parts of your bodies
or even your lives

without
asking permission
or saying
thank you,

for playing God
in the garden

and casually
cutting short
countless lives
because they

didn't suit
my narrow purposes.

Pardon me, plants,
for all the actions
I have taken
that harmed you,
directly or indirectly,

for all the car trips
and plane flights,
for all the things
I bought
but didn't
really need.

Pardon me,
plants,
for not speaking up
when I could have,

for standing by
in complicit silence
as your
ancient ones
were annihilated

by those
who couldn't
fully understand
what they
were destroying.

Pardon me,
plants—

after all,
I'm only
human.

An Earthly Reckoning

There were many times
I gently escorted insects
out of my house,

ducked down
to spare a spider web
that crossed my path,

or stepped carefully
to avoid crushing
a small beetle.

There were all the times
I made do
instead of buying new,

bundled up
instead of turning on
the heat,

used a clothesline
instead of a dryer,

and biked or rode transit
instead of driving.

There were all the times
I reduced, reused,
and recycled,

grew some of
my own food,

shelled out more
for organic produce or
recycled paper,

and avoided buying products
made of plastic
or made far away
(until that became
nearly impossible).

There were all the years
I dedicated
many of my waking hours
to causes that protect the Earth.

And yet, and yet…

There were also
all the times
I bought a meal
that I ate once
in a plastic container
that will last forever,

all the times
I purchased something
made far away
or that I didn't really need,

all the times
I drove my car
when I could have biked
or taken the bus,

all the times
I traveled by plane
for business or pleasure,
a carbon extravagance
our climate couldn't afford.

In some ways,
I have done my share

(some would say
much more)
to protect the Earth
and her creatures.

But I have also
done far more
than my share
of damage.

The fact that
that I never wanted
or intended
to cause this harm
doesn't erase the impacts.

The Earth on Life Support

These days,
being with the Earth
is like being
at the bedside
of a beloved grandmother
who is critically ill.

We love her
so much.

We hate
to see her
in pain.

We can't bear
the thought
of losing her.

We desperately
want to help,

yet what we're able to do
feels completely
inadequate.

It's almost
too much
to bear.

It's no wonder
that sometimes
we have to turn away.

Turn away
if you must.

Take breaks
when you need to.

Find the strength
to keep going
and then return
to her side.

Let her know
you're there.

Tell her how much
you love her.

Hold her hand.
Tell her stories.
Sing her songs.

Do what you can
to ease her suffering,
to bring her joy,

and help her
get the best care
available—

even if all this
will never
seem like enough.

Even if she doesn't
visibly respond,
she can hear you.

She can feel your love.

Now,
more than ever,
the Earth needs you.

The Color of Sunflowers

Lately I've been drawn
to the color
of sunflowers—

you know the one—

that deep, rich gold,

a gold with gravitas,

a gold with the power
to lift your spirits
out of the darkest depths
even if, say,

you were a year and a half
into a global pandemic
with no end in sight,

you had just learned
about a dear friend's
frightening diagnosis,

and vast stretches
of your beloved
home planet

were going up
in flames

as others
were drowning
in floods.

Who could blame you
for seeking out

a safe haven,
however small,

where you could
take refuge
for a few
blessed moments,

let your weary spirit
surrender
to the simple grace
of a sunny, golden flower,

and allow her
to work her magic
on you?

Walking Like a Poet

Sometimes
I walk
like a poet—

slowly,

mindfully,

as though I have
plenty of time
to marvel

at the many
small wonders
of the world...

the soft murmurs
of leaves
stirred
by a gentle breeze,

crimson blossoms
glowing
in the morning sun,

a shiny black beetle
trundling along
the path,

whose precious
yet humble life
will go on

because
I noticed
her presence.

Sometimes
I move
with awareness
that everything
is sacred,

and that my role
is nothing more—

and nothing less—

than to honor
that sacredness.

SUN AND RAIN

A Quest for Sunshine

Winter
in the woods.

Each morning,
a quest
for precious slivers
of sunlight

that have
miraculously
survived a journey
of millions of miles
from their birthplace

and navigated their way
through a dense thicket
of evergreens

to reach the plants
and animals
eagerly awaiting
their arrival
at the forest floor—
including me.

A patch of sun
large enough
to light my face
is a blessing,

one big enough
to warm my whole body
a revelation.

Every cell
sings Hallelujah!

Meeting the Morning Sun

Any moment now,
the morning sun
will arrive
on my small porch

for a brief visit
on his daily rounds.

As usual, he has
a full schedule,

an endless stream
of important engagements
around the clock.

Every plant,
every tree,
indeed everyone
and virtually
everything

depends on him
for their livelihood,
even for their lives.

Still, the sun,
having done this
for so many years,
makes it look easy.

He has learned
to hold
all this responsibility
lightly.

Celebrating the Sun

And on
the third day,
the sun came out,

and there was
great rejoicing
in the land.

Tears of joy
flowed,
grateful prayers
were spoken,
songs of jubilation
filled the air.

You would think
it had been
three weeks,
even three months,
not merely three days
since we had seen
the sun.

Perhaps
it is a blessing
that such a brief absence
can make the heart
grow so much fonder,

and inspire
new depths
of gratitude
for the formerly ordinary
miracles
of blue sky
and sunshine.

Second Sunrise

If I rise early
at this mountain
retreat center,

I can witness
the glorious moment
when the sun
crests the forested ridge
to the East

and bathes the valley
between us
with light—

a transformation
so sudden, profound,
and life-giving

that it can
truly be called
miraculous.

This alone
would be
more than enough,
this alone
could make my day.

Still, from my perch
on this steep slope,
I can amble downhill
for a few minutes
to a lower ridge

and experience
that miraculous moment

a second time
from a different
yet equally glorious
perspective.

I can be blessed
with a second sunrise—

just one of many
extraordinary gifts
of this mountain landscape.

Thirst

Precious
little rain
this year.

The plant people
are so thirsty.

Shrubs
turn brown
and shrivel;

trees
drop vast numbers
of leaves and needles,

knowing
there isn't
enough water

to keep them
all alive,

trying to save
the ones they can.

Meanwhile,
inside
my cozy
little house,

I can simply
turn a tap
and have
all the cool, clear water
I need—

plenty to drink,
to wash my dishes
and clothes,
to keep
my garden green—

even though
countless plants
and trees
in my community

are literally dying
of thirst.

How can
this be?

Before the First Drop Falls

How long
does it take
before thirsty plants
feel quenched
by the first rain
of the season?

Must they
wait patiently
for hours,
perhaps even days

as the water
gradually
wends its way
through the dry soil
to their eager roots?

Does feeling
the cool droplets
on their leaves
offer some respite
from their thirst,

a tantalizing taste
of the quenching
that will soon
be theirs?

Or do they sense
the rain coming
and begin
to celebrate

long before
the first drop falls?

This Changes Everything

After a long,
dry summer,

an early,
quenching rain.

Millions
of thirsty plants
breathe

a collective
sigh of relief.

This
changes
everything!

Warm and Dry

I give thanks
for the wisdom
of wool socks

that know how
to keep my feet warm
even when they're wet.

I worship
the wonders
of a soft fabric shell
that shapes itself
to my body

and follows
wherever I go,
keeping me dry inside.

I bow down
to the everyday magic
of a metal box that,
like a friendly genie,

generates heat
as soon as
I flick a small switch.

Small superpowers,
everyday marvels,
and ordinary alchemy

that keep me
warm and dry
even when it is
cold and wet
outside.

The Water Has Her Way With Me

My wool socks,
while still warm,
are decidedly not dry.

My leather boots
and nylon rain shell,
having valiantly resisted

the gentle
yet persistent advances
of the rain
for nearly two hours,

are beginning
to yield.

The water
is having her way
with me,

finding her way
to and through me.

TREES

Beauty and Music

The beauty
of bare branches.

The beauty
of lush green.

The music
of tree dances

and the stillness
in between.

Here in the Forest, I Feel the Ocean

In the midst
of the redwoods,

miles from
the edge
of the water,

I see and feel
the presence
of the ocean
all around me—

in the distant refrain
of her song,

a refreshing breeze
on a hot day,

the cool blanket of fog
that envelops the trees
many nights
and mornings,

and in the redwoods
themselves,

who rely on this fog
to nourish them
through the
dry summer months.

Here in the forest,
I see and feel the ocean
all around me.

Eight Views of a Redwood

Fibrous
red bark,

soft
yet strong.

Deep furrows
and canyons.

——-

Resting
on the Earth,

I gaze up
into branches

that touch
the sky.

——

Flying over
the mountains,

a dense canopy
of trees,

the few houses
and roads
below

barely visible.

——

A dark
and fertile world,

an underground universe
of living intelligence

feeding the roots,

feeding the trees.

——-

I lean into
my beloved.

His solid,
steady trunk
supports me.

I am not alone.

——

A tiny seed,
one of millions,
even billions.

Will it
have a chance
to grow?

——-

A young sapling
surrounded by
tall trees

sees what is
possible.

aspires
to greatness.

———-

An ancient tree

has seen
many things.

has deep wisdom
to share.

Who will
listen?

Meant To Be

I was meant
for this—

to root deeply
in the Earth

and reach high
into the sky,

to feel
the warm kiss
of sun,

the cool caress
of rain,

the fresh breath
of the sea,

to gather
all these gifts
and create life
for myself and others.

I was meant to live
to a ripe old age,

surrounded
by my children
and grandchildren,

to watch them grow
and share my stories.

I was meant to be
an elder.

I was not
meant to die
so you could have
a fence,
a deck,
or a better view.

I, too,
have dreams.

I, too,
have a destiny,

no less than
the humans
and the stars.

I am here
for a reason.

I was meant to be
an ancient
and mighty tree.

Grandmother Apple

Grandmother Apple,

I see your scarred
and weathered bark,

your gnarled
and twisted limbs.

Grandmother Apple,

I see your strong
and solid trunk,

your deep
and knowing roots,

your vibrant
green leaves

and exquisite
white blossoms.

Grandmother Apple,

scarred
and gnarled,

strong
and solid,

vibrant
and exquisite...

you are
more beautiful
than ever.

Spring Fashion Among the Apples

Spring
is here,

and it is
once again
customary,
indeed fashionable,

for even the most
gnarled
and ancient
apple trees

to be seen
out and about
in lavish gowns
of pink and white
blossoms
befitting
a young bride.

Only
the most
jaded eye

could fail
to appreciate
their enduring beauty.

TRUE LOVE

With Love

Walking barefoot
on the Earth

Each step
given
with love

Each step
received
with love

Beloved Redwood

Beloved redwood,
friend and teacher,
thank you
for giving so much
to so many…

fresh air,
shade and shelter,
beauty and inspiration,
more than words can say.

Beloved redwood,
friend and teacher,

thank you
for your deep
and eloquent teachings

on what it is
to be rooted,
to be balanced
between Earth and sky,
to give generously.

Beloved redwood,
friend and teacher,

thank you for letting me
lean into your trunk
and feel your support,

for allowing me
to call on you
for strength and guidance
even when you're far away.

Beloved redwood,
friend and teacher,

thank you for showing me
how to listen deeply,

for holding and healing me
in more ways
than human words
can express.

Beloved redwood,
beloved redwood,
beloved redwood!

Never Alone

Some would say
they went out alone,
but I wouldn't.

Some would say
they didn't see a soul,
but I wouldn't.

I would say
I went out
into the woods

and was surrounded
by friends and relations
every step of the way.

I would say
I was never alone
and never lonely.

Three Little Words

Sometimes
when I'm walking
in the woods,
I can't
contain myself.

I say
"I love you"
to almost everyone
I see...

"I love you
redwood,
madrone,
live oak,

I love you
sun,
sky,
stream."

It's so easy
to do.

It requires
only a few moments
and a bit of breath.

Yet those
three little words
make a big difference
to me...

and I think
to them, too.

Relationship Status

He said,
"I want to date you."

I said,
"I'm not dating."

He said,
"Your Facebook profile
says 'single.'"

I said,
"That's because
'married to the Earth'

wasn't included
as an option."

Smitten with a Kitten

Silky fur   A ready purr

Golden eyes   Slender thighs

Soft little paws   Sharp little claws

Simple grace   Enjoys her space

Beautiful markings   Never any barkings

Cute as a button   More appealing than mutton

Frequent stretches   Occasional retches

Just a bit of noise   A big bundle of joys

Never a bore   Always easy to adore

A champion sleeper   This one's a keeper

Trees Don't Mind

Trees don't mind
if you don't
have it all
figured out,

if you laugh
"too loud"
or cry
"too easily,"

if you
don't
quite
fit in.

Trees don't mind
if your eyes
teeth hair clothes
aren't perfect,

if your socks
don't match,

if you're a little
rough around
the edges.

Trees don't mind
where
you were born,

what color
your skin is,

what language
you speak.

Trees don't mind
if you have
a few more pounds

or a lot less hair
than you used to,

if you walk
with a limp
or a cane.

Trees don't mind
if you're more sensitive
than the average person—

truth be told,
they love it!

Trees
accept you
exactly
as you are.

She Had Me

"It's not
that cold,"
she said.

"It'll feel
so good,"
she said.

"You know
you want it,"
she said.

"You won't
regret it."

She had me
at the first "it."

Before my mind
has time to decide,

my body
has already
said yes,

my clothes are lying
in a happy jumble
on the stones,

and I have
entered into
her silky softness.

Her liquid embrace
envelops every inch
of my thirsty skin.

It's not
that cold.

It does
feel good.

I do
want it.

I don't
regret it.

Seduced again...
by the river.

EVERYDAY SPIRITUALITY

Full Stop

Sometimes
I am seized
by a powerful urge
to hold still—

I mean,
really still—

not doing
    or accomplishing
    anything,

not reading
    or watching
    anything,

not thinking
    or planning
    anything,

not letting
my mind
race forward

even as
my body
appears to
hold still—

not doing *anything*

but simply being

here.
right.
now.

Sometimes
nothing less
than a full stop
will do.

Things I Am Not Going to Do Today

There are
so many things

I am *not*
going to do today.

I am not
going to pen
an epic poem

or the great
American novel.

I am not
going to stop
a speeding
freight train

or leap
tall buildings
in a single bound.

I am not
going to run
a four-minute mile

or create
a five-minute miracle.

I am not
going to discover
the cure
for cancer

or even
the common cold.

I am not
going to walk
on water

or feed
the multitudes
with just
five loaves
and two fish.

I am not
going to
promise you

a quick fix
or a
miracle cure.

I *am*
going to
do my best

to be present
where I am,

open
to what comes,

and grateful
for what is.

That
would be
enough

of a miracle

for one day.

Thank You, Cold

Thank you, cold,
for teaching me

to be grateful
for warmth.

Thank you, clouds,
for teaching me

to be grateful
for sun.

Thank you, noise,
for teaching me

to be grateful
for quiet.

Thank you, tears,
for teaching me

to be grateful
for laughter.

Thank you, loss,
for teaching me

to be grateful
for what I have.

Thank you, death,
for teaching me

to be grateful
for life.

Living with Loss

I am learning
to live with loss,

learning that I can't
ever really
hold anything,

own anything,

or control anything—

not even
my life—

no more than
my small hands
can stop
a mighty waterfall,

or my
finite mind
can grasp
the vastness
of eternity.

But I'm
only human,
so I can't help
but try.

While It's Here

This patch
of sun

this sip
of water

this ripe
apple

this breath
of air

this healthy
body

this entire
life

is available
for a
limited time.

I remind myself
to cherish it
while it's here.

Count Your Blessings

Count
your blessings

again
and again,

including
the seemingly
ordinary ones,

those that are
all too easy
to overlook
if you
have them,

and
all too painful
to lack
if you don't—

a roof
over your head,

water
to drink

and food
to eat,

legs
that can walk

and eyes
that can see,

all the parts
of your body
that keep
showing up

day after day,
year after year,

in sickness
and in health—

the seemingly
ordinary blessings

that are actually
quite extraordinary.

Green Wave

It's as though
the Universe
was saying,

"I know, that was
a tough afternoon.
I'm going to
make this evening
a little easier
for you.

So, here's a green light,
and another,
and another,
and another..."

All through town,
the green wave continued,
each light turning green
as I approached,

the path opening up
before me in a way
I have never experienced
in decades of driving
this often-congested
stretch of road.

This minor miracle
lifted my spirits
like you wouldn't believe—

or maybe
you would.

Pulling Weeds, Not Pulling Weeds

Pulling weeds.

Not pulling weeds.

Thinking about
pulling weeds.

Thinking about
not pulling weeds.

Thinking about
pulling weeds
more than
not thinking about it.

Thinking about
not wanting to
keep thinking about
pulling weeds.

Becoming obsessed
with not wanting to
think about
pulling weeds.

Then, meditating
on pulling weeds
and not pulling weeds.

Meditating
on attachment
to thinking
about pulling weeds

and aversion
to thinking

about pulling weeds.

Thoughts about
pulling weeds
arise.

Thoughts about
not pulling weeds
arise.

Ah, the mind—
so busy
with what
it is not
even doing!

Things to Do on a Sunday Morning

Wake up.
Smile.
Breathe.
Repeat.

Watch sunlight
stream through
the windows.

Listen
to birds sing.

Smile.
Breathe.
Repeat.

Get up
and make
a cup of tea.

Go back
to bed.

Listen
to birds sing
some more.

Savor
this moment

of not having
to go anywhere
or do anything,

of simply being.

Watch patches
of morning sun
migrate slowly
across your room.

They are
in no hurry.

There is
nowhere
they would
rather be.

All the Time in the World

What a gift
it is
not to hurry,

to do
at least
a few things

as though
I have
plenty
of time,

as though
I have
all the time
in the world.

Four Days of Retreat

For four days,
I didn't have to
answer the phone—

there was
no phone.

For four days,
I didn't have to
watch the clock—

there was
no clock.

For four days,
I didn't have to
look both ways

before crossing
the street—

there was
no street.

For four
blessedly simple days,

I didn't have to
hurry
to do anything
or go anywhere—

I was always
exactly
where I needed
to be.

Returning to the Well

If I do not
return
to the well,

how
can I
quench
my thirst?

If I do not
return
to the well,

how
can I
have
enough water
to share?

Again
and again,
I return
to the well.

I drink deeply.

I am quenched.

And I
have plenty
of water
to share.

THE NATURE OF CREATION

The Seeds of Words

I release words
on to the page
like windblown seeds,

never knowing
how far
they will travel

or where
they will land.

Writing, Like Breathing

Writing,
like breathing,

has a
natural
rhythm,

flows in
and out,

releases
what is
stale,

brings in
what is
fresh,

weaves
invisible threads
of connection,

is essential
to my
survival.

The Unknown Poet

For most
of my life,
I had no idea

there was
a poet
inside me,

just waiting for
the opportunity
to make
her presence known.

She was
so quiet,

and I was
so busy

that I
didn't hear
a thing.

Learning to Be a Poet

I am
learning
to be a poet.

My school
is out among
the forests
and fields,

my teachers
are trees
and birds,
streams
and stones,

and the poems
themselves.

Mostly,
they teach me
to listen.

After
a ten-year
apprenticeship,

I am still
a novice.

My Poetic License

I have a poetic license,
and I'm learning
how to use it.

I don't employ it
to stretch the truth
or to embroider
elaborate, epic tales.

I invoke it
for something
more singular
and precious,

more essential
to the making
of a poem—

to grant myself
permission

to step away
from the clamor
of daily demands

long enough to hear
the deeper currents
flowing beneath
the surface,

the soft voices
of new poems
asking
to be born.

Going to Work

"Mommy's going
to work now,"
I say to my inner poet,

with a deliberate lightness
in my voice
that doesn't match
what I feel
in my heart.

"OK, mommy!"
she says,
matching
my attempt
at brightness,

while her eyes
beg me
to stay.

Yet we both know
I can't,
at least not today.

We've done this
so many times.

We know
we'll get through it.

And it's
still hard.

The Poet in Hiding

My poet
is in hiding,

sequestered
in an undisclosed location

so deep inside me
that even I
don't know
where to find her.

She is determined
to stay there
until it's safe
to come out,

watching me
closely
for the signs.

She is prepared
to wait
for a long time.

I pray
she won't
have to.

An Open Door

Dear poems,

I am here.

Where are you?

Are you nearby?

I think I can
hear you
breathing.

If you want
to come in,

my door
is open.

You are
always
welcome.

And of course,
you will be free
to come and go
as you please.

I know how
you treasure
your freedom.

The Blessing of the Table Saw

And so it came to pass
that on the third day
the neighbor brought forth
his table saw,

and it was
not so good,

for the forest rang out
with the harsh whine
of metal grinding
through wood,

and a place
that had been
a peaceful sanctuary
became something different
for a time.

The nearby poet,
fervently seeking quiet,
was sorely tempted
to judge her neighbor
for the not-so-joyful noise
he was making.

Truth be told,
she had a few uncharitable,
some would say
un-Christian thoughts
about the sound of the saw,

yet she was not
so vexed
that she would wish
her fellow man harm.

And so
she blessed him
in his labors,

and prayed
that they be
completed safely
and with all
his fingers intact.

And the poet saw
that after two days
of mostly unbroken quiet
in the forest,

even the jarring sound
of a table saw
could become
the genesis
of a new poem.

And she saw
that it was good.

GETTING PERSONAL

Chocolate Before Breakfast

Before breakfast
is an eminently
agreeable time

to enjoy
a small square
of dark chocolate.

My taste buds,
barely awake,
still stretching
and yawning,

are thrilled
to find themselves
suddenly transported
into joyful alertness.

My palate,
as yet uncluttered
with the myriad flavors
of the day,

has ample space
to savor
the delectable sensations.

My somewhat
sensitive system,
which would be
catapulted
into complete chaos

by the complex
chemical cascade
of a cup of coffee,

can absorb
and appreciate
a modest morsel
of chocolate,

which offers
just enough
stimulation
to excite

but not enough
to overwhelm.

Cleaning the House of Memory

Why is it
that countless memories
of seemingly trivial events

are stored for years,
even decades,
although I have
no particular use
for them,

while mountains of
cherished memories
and vast troves
of useful information

are discarded
almost immediately,
with no apparent regard
for their value?

It's as though
a ruthless and capricious
house cleaner

storms through
my memories
multiple times a day,

randomly tossing them
into boxes marked
"long-term storage,"
"short-term storage,"

or (with alarming frequency)
"destroy immediately."

Part of me
wants to scream,

"Stop!
Those are
precious!
I might
need them
some day!"

Another part
is ready
to let them go.

Watching My Neighbors Walk

I watch
the couple
across the street
stroll along
the sidewalk.

I am struck
by how
they walk,
how unusual
it is.

They move
as though
they have
plenty of time—

as though
there are
no deadlines looming,

meetings
to attend,

or piles
of laundry to wash.

They move
as though
they are at a
seaside resort
on a balmy
summer day,

meandering
along the shore

after a good night's sleep
and a leisurely brunch,

soaking up
the sun,
breathing
the fresh sea air,

pausing to admire
the plump brown loaves
in the bakery window,

the graceful curves
of hand-crafted bowls
at the artisans' cooperative.

They walk
as though
there is no hurry,

nothing
more pressing
to attend to

than simply
savoring the moment
and finding
a good place
for dinner.

They move
as though
the world
is their oyster,

and they have
all the time
in the world
to enjoy its pearls.

I, too,
would like
to move like that.

And maybe,
just maybe,
I can.

Beginning to Know a Place

I've been
in this place
just long enough
to know

where the first rays
of morning sun
will slant
through the windows,

just long enough
to know

which drawer
holds the spoons,

which floorboards
will groan when
I step on them,

and which ones
can bear my weight
without complaining.

I've been here
just long enough
to know

which birds
will sing
before sunrise,

and where
I can walk
at night

to see
the fewest artificial lights
and the most abundant stars.

I am just beginning
to know this place,

and already
it is almost time
to leave.

Listening to My Back

My back
is speaking,

calling to me softly
through quiet
little twinges.

If I listen
to these whispers,
then it won't
have to shout.

Part of Me

I miss the part of me
that wrote poetry—

I haven't seen her
for a while.

I miss the part of me
that smiled and laughed
readily,

that sang
while she washed
the dishes,

that slept
through the night
and woke up
feeling rested.

I miss the part of me
that had time

to plant
in her garden,

cook dinners
from scratch,

offer a shoulder
to cry on—

time for
a thousand
small kindnesses
toward herself
and others.

I miss the part of me
that asked herself
what she wanted to do
and listened
for the answer,

that sometimes
spent all day
quietly wandering
through forests and fields,
attuning to
the rhythms of nature.

So many parts of me
buried under an
avalanche of work.

I can still
hear them
breathing.

If I act quickly,
I can save them.

The Question

Even though I feel
quite comfortable
out on the trail
"alone,"

even though
I am strong
and resourceful
and would not make
an easy target,

even though
in decades
of solo hiking

I have never
been threatened,
much less harmed—
not once.

Despite all this,
whenever
I pass a man,

no matter
how kind
and gentle
he looks,

part of me
still wonders,

part of me
still asks,

"am I safe?"

Two Stores

I bumped into a friend
in the grocery store.

After we
exchanged greetings,

she gestured at her cart,
laden with dozens
of items,

and lamented
that she was only
half-way done,

because she had to go
to two different stores
to get everything she needed.

I briefly contemplated
the shelves around us,
overflowing with
thousands of items,

and the ease with which
we could stroll down the aisles
and gather everything
we need for the week
in a matter of minutes.

In my mind's eye,
I contrasted that scene
with images of

people toiling in the fields
all day under the hot sun,

walking for miles
to a village market,

and subsisting on
a few staples
through a long, cold winter.

It seemed to me
that going to two stores
wasn't such a great burden,

that even for those of us
of modest means,
food-gathering
in our country
is now easier
than it has been

for most people
in most places
at most times
in human history.

But I kept
these thoughts
to myself.

Homeland

In a way
you could say
I am a displaced person.

Thousands of miles
and a vast ocean
separate me

from my birthplace,
extended family,
and original
mother tongue.

Yet despite all this,
I feel deeply rooted

in my
adopted homeland
at the edge
of the Pacific Ocean,

where I
have found
a friendly
second mother tongue,

loving extended family
in both the human
and more-than human worlds,

and a place
I am immensely grateful
to call home.

Even Then

Even when
I forget to ask,
they are with me.

Even when
I don't call
their names,
they hear me
and come to my side.

Even when
I think
I'm walking alone,
they are walking
beside me.

Even when
the burdens
feel unbearably heavy,
they are lightening the load.

Even when
I forget to thank them,
they keep coming back.

And when I remember
to call on them,
to notice their presence,
and to give thanks,

my spirit guides
are even
more fully there

and I am
more fully here.

I Give Thanks to My Ancestors

I give thanks
to my ancestors

for going before

for finding the way

for continuing
an often bent

yet never
fully broken line

that allowed me
to be here today.

I give thanks
to my ancestors

for the myriad
gifts and strengths

they passed on
to their children
and their children's children

who became
my parent's parents.

I give thanks
to my ancestors

for all that
they loved
and sometimes lost,

for all that they sought
and sometimes found,

for all the seeds
they planted,
sometimes in barren soil,

for all the dreams
deferred, denied,
or realized.

I give thanks
to my ancestors

for all they survived,
for all they passed on—

even the wounds,
because those wounds
held seeds
of profound learning
and healing

that sometimes
found fertile soil,
took root, and flowered.

Those seeds
and that flowering
are not just for us—

they are for all
who came before,

all who are
here now,

and all those
yet to come.

POEMLETS

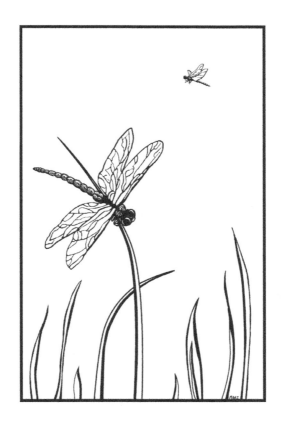

Smooth
stream
slipping

Cool
water
rippling

Dragonflies
glinting
in the sun

—

Distant light
of stars

travels
long and far

to kiss
the tops
of trees.

—

By the edge
of the water

at the edge
of the day

on the edge
of not knowing

yet still
finding
your way.

I am immersed
in the songs
of birds.

My grateful spirit sings.

—

Birds sing above.

Creek sings below.

In the middle,
I listen.

—

Hummingbird
sits on
her perch.

I sit on mine.

We share
a moment.

—

I come here
to listen

I come here
to see

I come
to remember

what it is
to be me.

Sand,
I see you.

So solid
yet so soft.

Each grain
has traveled far.

Each has a story
to tell.

—

A hot day.

Every sliver
of shade

every breath
of breeze

a blessing.

—

"Rain tomorrow,"

I say
to the plants
in my garden.

But of course,
they already
know that.

Here among
the trees,

there's
so much room
for me.

There's
so much room
to heal.

—

Every day
is a gift,

and out here
they are
exquisitely
wrapped!

—

Going somewhere
and truly being
somewhere

are entirely
different things.

—

Just enough sun
to be warm.

Just enough shade
to be cool.

Just enough breeze

to be refreshing.

Just enough tears
to be happy.

—

It only takes
a day of gray

to remind me
that sunlight
is a miracle.

—

Tall trees.

Wild wind.

Let's dance!

—

True quiet
is so much more

than just
an absence
of noise.

—

I like to
slow down
quickly

and speed up
slowly.

The world
is my oyster,

and I am grateful
to be one
of its many pearls.

—

Life is short—
and we have
no idea
how long.

—

Spring,
like life,
so precious
and fleeting—

I want to cherish
the blossoms
while they are
still here.

NATURE PRACTICES

Of the many gifts my parents gave me, time in nature has been one of the most essential and enduring. Our family hikes and camping trips brought me joy, taught me to feel at home in the great outdoors, and instilled a lifelong love for the natural world.

As an adult, this love affair found more varied expressions as I ventured farther afield and explored a wide range of outdoor activities. I backpacked through granite mountains, rafted wild and scenic rivers, cross-country skied by moonlight, and kayaked with dolphins and whales. I encountered many beautiful places and natural wonders and had some of the best times of my life—and yet I had no idea how much I was missing.

How could this be? I was relating to nature the way my culture had trained me to—as an outdoor gym and scenic backdrop. When I hiked, I focused on getting from point A to point B and missed many of the points in between. I almost always went out with other people and talked much of the time. I rarely engaged directly with more-than-human beings, treating them like attractive wallpaper—not friends and relations. I loved nature and thought we had a great relationship but didn't realize how much more was possible.

Then, 11 years ago, I was going through a major life transition and seeking guidance. I felt called to go out into nature and listen. What I heard was clear and compelling. Nature said: "Slow down. Hold still. Pay attention. Listen. We are alive and intelligent, and we have much to share with those who will listen." Nature's voice infiltrated my being like a soft rain on thirsty ground, and I knew I had found the wise guidance I sought. And needed.

Following nature's lead, I made a few key changes. Instead of planning walks with friends, I went out solo and attuned to nature's rhythms. Rather than fixating on getting exercise or reaching a destination, I ambled slowly or settled into one place to listen. Instead of treating more-than-human beings like part of the backdrop, I approached them with greater respect for their wisdom. I sat by a flowing creek or leaned into the trunk of a tree, intentionally opening myself to whatever wanted to come through… and what I received surpassed my wildest expectations.

I experienced extraordinary depths of peace and communion with Earth and Spirit, far beyond anything I had known before. I began receiving poetry spontaneously and effortlessly, as though I had tapped an abundant wellspring. Although I was spending little time with other humans, I felt less alone and more supported than ever. I had discovered a window to a world of connection and co-creation with nature that had always been there yet was hidden in plain sight.

Over the past 10 years, I've been sharing what I learned through experiential programs in the forests near my home. The magic that unfolds when participants open to a deeper connection with nature is palpable, and the common themes they describe are inspiring: profound peace, heightened awareness of beauty and wonder, fresh insights, and a sense of belonging and oneness. Even those who have spent extensive time outdoors experience it in new ways.

Do we really need to teach people how to connect with nature? I say yes. Why? Because our modern Western culture systematically conditions even those of us who love nature to think and act as though we're separate from it. When we go out into natural settings, we are weighed down by habits of disconnection we don't even know we're carrying. Most of us follow unwritten rules that we've been trained in almost since birth: stay busy, keep moving, keep talking, don't fraternize with the natives.

I know first-hand that we can have amazing experiences and receive far-reaching benefits from time outdoors even if we follow all these rules. Still, they create an invisible barrier between us and the deeply healing connection with nature that is our birthright.

The good news is that we are wired to connect with nature, and this bond is readily strengthened. A few simple shifts in our awareness and actions can make a world of difference. When we're out in wild places, these shifts include slowing down, being quiet, opening our senses, and directly engaging with more-than-human beings. In our everyday lives, they involve noticing the presence of nature and finding simple ways to say "yes" to it.

Whatever the setting, approaching beings and places in nature as friends and relations is one key to a more respectful relationship. While it may seem like a stretch within today's nature-disconnected culture, this view has been common for most of our history on planet Earth. Our kinship with nature is innate, healthy, and readily rekindled if we give it a chance.

This is partly just a change in perspective, to seeing and naming more-than-human beings and wild places we care about as friends or loved ones. Our circle of friends might include trees, lakes, and trails that are special to us, that we return to again and again, and would leave a hole in our heart if they were destroyed. Making friends in the natural world is simple and rewarding. It's mostly about being curious, paying attention, and finding ways to communicate. Small things like sitting quietly, engaging through touch, or saying "hello" or "thank you" can go a long way.

Our words matter. Changing just a few of them can help us step out of regarding more-than-human beings as objects and into affirming that they are intelligent, sentient beings who deserve our respect. A few examples: saying "he/she/they" instead of "it," "who is that bird?" instead of "what is that bird?," "more-than-human beings" instead of "other species," "my tree friend" instead of "a tree," "I love you, ocean" instead of "I love the ocean." Our choice of words can express and reinforce our own respect and kinship as well as inspire others to join us.

Connecting with nature matters too. It's not just about scenic views and enjoyable afternoons. It's not just about reducing stress and enhancing health. It offers a direct path to deeper experiences that are essential to our well-being yet often hard to find in the frantic swirl of modern life. In nature, we can immerse ourselves in peace and beauty, slow down, and breathe. We're reminded of what is healthy and thriving, and that, despite everything, life goes on. We can experience being part of something much greater than ourselves and touch the sacred. The more open and present we are, the more we can receive.

And the benefits are not just for us. Both modern research and millennia of Indigenous wisdom make it clear that connecting with nature helps us be our best selves and treat others better. Extensive research documents that contact with nature makes us more flexible, cooperative, and creative. The effects are so powerful that even images of nature indoors or views outside a window reduce conflict and enhance performance in schools and workplaces. The effects also go far beyond what we know how to measure. As traditional cultures all over the world have recognized, nature offers a vast repository of wisdom, and listening to it is essential to understanding who we are and how to live.

There are two basic keys to nurturing your relationship with the natural world amidst the challenges of modern life: finding simple ways to connect with the Earth wherever you are, and knowing how to open to a deeper communion when you are in natural settings. This chapter can help you do both.

These practices are designed to help you make connecting with nature, well, second nature. I've organized them into two sections, one for natural settings and one for daily life. They are designed for busy people, and many can be done in just a minute or two, although giving them more time and space will allow you to have richer experiences and receive more benefits. Most can be done either alone or with others and are appropriate in a variety of settings. Some are adapted from my first book, *Poems of Earth and Spirit*.

These activities are akin to recipes based on simple, healthy ingredients that can be combined in various ways with delicious results. It may help to think of them as a menu of options. You don't have to "order" them all at once—or ever. Notice which entice you, try one or two, and see if you feel called to continue those practices or to sample others.

As with any practices, starting small, linking them to regular activities, and reminding yourself to do them will help you make them part of the fabric of your life. Reflecting, sharing with someone, or journaling can allow you to integrate the benefits and inspire you to keep practicing. I encourage you to follow your intuition, go at your own pace, and honor your own rhythms... just as nature would want it.

16 Ways to Deepen Your Connection with Nature

These practices are designed for natural settings and moments when you have more time and space to be present. They also can be used in home gardens, city parks, or other environments that combine natural and human-made elements.

Senses and Presence

1. Take time to arrive. When you enter a natural setting, pause to notice where you are and allow yourself to arrive. Sit or stand quietly. Enjoy a few deep breaths and feel your feet on the Earth. Open your awareness to your surroundings, absorbing the sights and sounds. What calls to you? How does it feel to arrive in that place? You may want to give thanks or set an intention for your time there.

2. Open your senses. Tuning into your senses allows you to experience the beauty and wonder of nature more fully. Try focusing on one sense at a time, savoring the delicious sights, sounds, scents, and textures of nature. Enjoy the gentle sounds of birdsong, moving water, or leaves whispering in the breeze, drinking it in as you might an exquisite musical performance. Or try exploring a flower, tree, or small patch of Earth with all your senses. Closing your eyes will heighten your awareness of other senses.

3. Get in touch. Mindful touch brings you into the moment and creates a more embodied connection. Explore the varied sensations of leaves, bark, stone, and water with your hands, feet, or your whole body. Going barefoot is a ticket to intimate encounters with nature and some surprisingly delightful sensations. Direct contact with the Earth (known as Earthing or grounding) also balances your body's electromagnetic energy. Touching soil, stone, sand, and water all have this effect.

4. Be present. As you hike or move through a landscape, practice bringing mindful awareness to your surroundings and your experience in the moment. Notice what draws your attention and lean in for a closer look. See how fully present you can be with a single leaf, a flowing creek, or the warmth of the sun on your skin. When your mind wanders, gently bring it back to what you are sensing in the moment. The more present you are, the more you will receive from time in nature.

Motion and Stillness

5. Discover the power of the pause. When you're outside, pause occasionally to take in your surroundings. Stop, look, and listen. Allow the beauty of nature to stop you in your tracks, for a moment, a minute, or maybe more.

6. Be still. Go to a peaceful place in nature where you feel safe, and sit or lie still for at least five minutes. (You may want to bring a small cloth or pad to sit or lie on.) Open your senses and awareness to your surroundings and give yourself as fully as possible to that place in that moment. Allow your eyes to close for at least part of the time. Let yourself be held and supported by the natural world. Enjoy simply being in that special place, creating peace in yourself and on the Earth.

7. Go quietly, or go solo. Enjoy a silent hike, either on your own or with a companion. Instead of talking or listening to music, tune into the sights and sounds of nature and what you notice in the moment. You may want to be silent for part of your time together and then share about what you experienced.

Or try going solo. It's one of the best ways to be more aware of your environment and more fully present with nature and yourself. If this feels uncomfortable to you, try going "solo-ish" by keeping a short distance between you and your companion.

8. Let the land lead you. Meander through a natural setting without a particular destination or agenda. Open your awareness to your surroundings, noticing what draws your attention and where you feel called to go (or stop). Engage directly with the beings and elements around you through your senses, presence, and/or words. Enter into an embodied conversation with the living world, letting your body language affirm connection rather than separation. Move *with* the land, rather than simply moving *through*.

9. Expand your range of motion. Moving mindfully or creatively allows you to engage with nature with greater aliveness, creativity, and joy. Explore various ways of walking: barefoot, slowly, or very quietly, being present with each step. Try moving less like a train on a track and more like a curious animal—climb a tree, wander through a stream bed, or move on all fours. Or explore dancing or freeform movement outdoors, letting the movements of trees, grasses, clouds, and water inspire yours.

Kinship and Communication

10. Connect with one being. Wander quietly through a natural area, noticing where you feel intuitively called to go. Be open to the possibility of connecting deeply with a plant, creek, boulder, or any aspect of nature, and notice when you feel like you have found them. Get to know this being through your senses, moving around them and touching them if you can (after asking permission). After a while, settle into stillness, perhaps sitting or lying down near your nature partner. Open yourself to them and listen for as long as you like, and thank them before you move on.

11. Make friends and relations. Making friends with more-than-human beings is easier than you might think. Notice the beings and places you are instinctively drawn to and give yourself a chance to get to know them, preferably one on one. Sit with them, speak to them, listen to them. Explore what it's like to approach them as sentient beings who are potential friends and teachers, rather than as objects. Keep in touch and tend the connection. You may be surprised by the depth of friendship that can blossom.

12. Listen deeply. Listening is essential to all relationships, including with the natural world. Practice being quiet inside and out, allowing nature to speak to you. You can ask a question, create an intention, or be open to whatever comes. Consider sitting down with a pen and journal to discover what wants to come through. See if you can listen not just with your ears, but also with your body, heart, and spirit. Nature holds abundant wisdom for those who listen.

13. Use your words, and go beyond words. Try speaking a few words to more-than-human beings and see what you notice. "Hello," "thank you," and "I love you" are good places to start. Feel free to have a longer dialogue through speaking or writing, or step into their roots or paws and speak in their voice. This can be a powerful way to receive wisdom and medicine from nature.

Also explore nonverbal ways to communicate with the natural world, including through awareness, listening, body language, touch, and offerings. Notice what you feel intuitively called to do and what you sense when you reach out. You may receive communication from nature through sensations, energy, feelings, words, images, inner knowing, or in other forms. It may be immediate and clearly apparent, or subtle and revealed over time.

14. Pour your heart out. Find a quiet place in nature where you feel safe, and speak or write about whatever you need to express. Pour your heart out, without holding back or editing yourself. Share your deepest, unvarnished truths, as though you are with one of your most trustworthy friends (because, guess what, you are!) You can write or speak directly to the Earth, a tree, another more-than-human being, or an ancestor or spirit guide—or just let the words flow through and land wherever they may. While this may feel awkward at first, it quickly becomes more comfortable if you give it a chance.

15. Give thanks. We receive many gifts from nature. Expressing gratitude helps us notice and appreciate what we're given and cultivates a more respectful relationship with the natural world. You can say "thank you" through awareness, words, a gesture, or giving back. Naming names is good! ("Thank you, oak trees, for...") Developing simple customs like giving thanks as you get up from a lunch spot or complete a hike will help you make a habit of gratitude and inspire others to join you. You can also give back to a special place by removing trash, donating, and/or volunteering.

16. Honor the sacred. Reverence for nature is one of the most direct paths to experience the sacred, one that deepens our innate bond with the Earth and all life. You don't need to follow a script or go about it a certain way. Whatever you believe, approaching with respect, being present, feeling awe, and giving thanks can be gateways to the sacred.

There is tremendous power in authentic, heartfelt blessings and ceremonies, even very simple and spontaneous ones. You can honor a special being or place in nature with a song, poem, prayer, or words of gratitude. Or you might make a symbolic offering or create a ceremony to thank and bless a tree, river, or mountain, on your own or with others. If you have a regular spiritual or mindfulness practice, try bringing it outside and welcoming the natural world into your practice, or including nature in your practice wherever you are.

12 Ways to Connect with Nature Wherever You Are

These practices offer simple ways to appreciate nature in built environments and to integrate mindful nature connection with everyday activities. Many can be done in just a few minutes. Some can be used indoors, even in windowless buildings!

1. Start where you are. Notice how the natural world is part of your everyday life, even in the midst of a city—in food, water, plants, animals, seasonal cycles, your own body, and more. Also notice which aspects of nature you are instinctively drawn to and find ways to say "yes" to them, even for just a few moments. Simply bringing awareness to the presence of nature will strengthen your connection with it.

2. Bring the outside in. Having green plants or nature images in a room beautifies the space and reminds you of your relationship to the natural world. It also reduces stress, enhances performance, and supports healing. This is especially valuable in rooms without windows or natural views.

3. Look up and out. We all need breaks to stay effective. Gazing at a green plant or a pleasing view, even for just a minute, restores attention and focus. Looking out a window for longer periods of time to watch the sun rise or snow fall, observe birds feeding, or mindfully connect with a tree helps you attune to daily and seasonal cycles and get to know your natural neighbors even while you're indoors.

4. Step outside. For a brief refresher, step outside and enjoy a few deep breaths. Take in the sights and sounds, noticing what draws your attention in a pleasing way. Or bring regular activities like meals, family time, reading, or meditation into nature or outdoors—even if it's just on your front porch or in your backyard.

5. Unplug. To reduce stress and anxiety, take breaks from electronic devices, especially when you're outdoors. Turn off or silence your device, stow it away, or leave it behind. Enjoy observing the world around you, tuning into the presence of natural beauty.

6. Listen to your body. Your body is part of nature and listening to it connects you with natural wisdom that can keep you safe, healthy, and happy. Check in with your body periodically to notice what you need (food, water, a break, movement?) You can bring awareness to your body by pausing, closing your eyes, placing your hands on your body, and/or tuning into your breath or physical sensations. Also notice what kind of environments you are instinctively drawn to and which ones leave you feeling relaxed, nourished, or enlivened.

7. Move it! Movement supports your health and happiness in myriad ways. Find opportunities to move that work for your body and bring you joy. You don't have to run a marathon or climb a mountain—a walk around the block, a brief dance, or gentle stretches can make a difference. You may want to explore moving intuitively, without any agenda, by tuning to your body and noticing how you feel called to move. Taking your movement outdoors multiplies the benefits and will leave you feeling more revitalized, especially if you choose settings with abundant plants and trees, visible water, or other natural beauty.

8. Visit nature in your mind's eye. Visualizing yourself in a special place in nature helps you stay connected with it and even provides some of the same health benefits as actually being there. Sit or lie down in a quiet, comfortable spot. Close your eyes, breathe deeply, and travel in your mind's eye to your special place. Notice what you see, hear, and sense, soaking up the natural goodness. When you're ready to come back, give thanks to the place and then transition gently by noticing your breath and present-time sensations and moving slowly into whatever is next. Another option is to use a guided meditation recording that features nature imagery or poetry, or to make your own.

9. Cultivate nature allies. All aspects of the natural world have wisdom and medicine to share. Developing respectful, reciprocal relationships with them allows us to receive guidance and healing from nature wherever we are. You may invite a particular being or aspect of nature to work with you, or ask for an ally to come to you and see who appears. Calling on allies regularly and/or speaking or writing in their voice will deepen your connection with them and your capacity to access nature's wisdom. Remember to honor and thank your nature allies for their support and find ways to give back.

10. Give thanks. Expressing gratitude for gifts we receive from the Earth helps us enjoy and appreciate them and fosters a more respectful relationship with nature. You might pause to give thanks for the food on your plate, a sunset, or a lovely flower. Consider keeping a gratitude journal, or writing a thank-you letter to the Earth or a being or place in nature that is special to you. Expressing your gratitude will nourish you and the natural world.

11. Connect and conserve. You can connect with nature and protect it at the same time through daily choices that get you outside, use human and green power, and reduce resource consumption. A few examples: walking or biking rather than driving, using a clothesline instead of a dryer, gardening, composting, and eating local, seasonal, and/or organic foods. Linking your daily actions with love for the Earth makes them more satisfying and meaningful.

12. Make it part of your day. Integrating your nature practices with regular events or times of day makes them more doable and helps you remember to do them. You might pause to greet a tree that you walk by every day, visit your garden for a few minutes when you come home, or thank the plants and animals who made your dinner possible. Consider this an essential wellness practice to integrate into your day, like eating meals or brushing your teeth. A little bit of mindful nature connection, even in the midst of a city, can go a surprisingly long way.

LAST WORDS

Many Thanks!

It takes a village to birth a book, in this case one supported by a larger community in the natural world. I am deeply grateful to all those who contributed to this volume:

The trees, plants, animals, streams, and other more-than-human beings who co-created these poems... I couldn't have done it without you!

Special places that have been beloved friends and creative collaborators for many years, especially the Santa Cruz Mountains, the North Coast of Santa Cruz, the Big Sur Coast, the Yuba River, and the Sierra Nevada Range. Thank you for always giving me exactly what I needed and more!

The Vajrapani Institute, Ben Lomond Quaker Center, and Suzanne Morrow for the abundant gifts that come from silent retreat on peaceful land, including the birth of many of these poems.

Mária Kersey for adding so much beauty to this book through her exquisite illustrations, being a joy to work and play with, generously donating her time, taking the author photo, and 30-plus years of loving friendship.

Martha Bullen for the perfect subtitle, skillful editing, and friendly expert advice on many aspects of book creation and publishing.

Mary Reynolds-Thompson for applying her editing wizardry to key sections of prose.

The volunteers who edited, reviewed, or proofed sections of text: Greg Thrush, Jared Jones, Joel Wallock, Julia Gratton, Mitchell Goldstein, Nina Siedenburg, Steve Lustgarden, and Tierra Ortiz-Rodriguez. Thank you for making this a better book through your reflections and corrections!

Extra special thanks to superstar volunteers Annie Scavone McEnroe and Tamara Myers, who reviewed every single poem and almost all the prose and offered infusions of enthusiasm and words of encouragement just when I needed them!

Jeremy Thornton for another fantastic cover design (three for three!), Kazutoki for the stunning cover image, and the pictured leaves for sharing their splendor.

Debora Seidman for guiding me to new places in my writing and nourishing my creativity through her Sacred Writing Circles.

Ariana Candell of The Earthbody Institute for being a kind and generous friend and collaborator, and helping my poems travel the world and meet friendly people.

Everyone who has told me about how my work has touched your life, and everyone who has believed in and encouraged me.

The spirit guides and nature allies who support me every step of the way, even when I don't notice.

Finally, boundless gratitude to my ancestors for making it possible for me to be here and to write these words, and to my parents for giving me so much, including a deep love of nature.

About the Author

Kai Siedenburg is a nature connection guide, Ecotherapist, and poet who is passionate about helping people connect with the healing power of nature for the benefit of all beings. A pioneer in integrating nature awareness and mindfulness as a path to mind-body wellness, she offers individual sessions, group programs, and consulting services through Our Nature Connection.

Her approach is rooted in deep listening to nature and informed by 30-plus years of experience developing innovative educational programs and extensive practice in mindfulness, holistic healing, and creative expression. Kai's life and work are woven around four golden threads: love for people, love for the Earth, desire for deep connection, and a strong call to contribute.

She lives on the territory of the Awaswas-speaking Uypi people (now represented by the Amah Mutsun Tribal Band), where the mountains meet the sea in Santa Cruz, California. Kai loves to find herself out on the Earth, in her garden, in water, or on the dance floor, and aspires to touch the Earth with her hands or bare feet every day.

She is also the author of *Poems of Earth and Spirit: 70 Poems and 40 Practices to Deepen Your Connection with Nature* and *Space Between the Stones: Poetry and Practices for Connecting with Nature, Spirit, and Creativity*. Both volumes were selected as finalists for Next Generation Indie Book Awards.

Learn more about her story at OurNatureConnection.com

About the Illustrator

Mária Kersey is an artist and public high school teacher based in Santa Cruz, California. Childhood experiences exploring the outdoors seeded her lifelong love of nature. Summer camping trips with her parents and brother inspired her to continue these adventures as a young adult with solo excursions backpacking in British Columbia and camping in Arizona. Later, as a mom and teacher, she hiked the Sierras with her sons and organized photography trips to Yosemite for her students. Being in nature enriches her life and relationships with family and friends—including the author of this book.

Mária began her artistic career as an apprentice potter at eleven years old, taught ceramics as a teenager, and later earned a degree in graphic design with a focus on illustration. She creates with diverse materials and modes, including woodworking, construction, drafting, tile masonry, photography, gardening, ceramics, painting, drawing, computer graphics, singing, and playing acoustic music. On her days off from teaching, she works for the local California State Parks.

About the Amah Mutsun Land Trust

The Amah Mutsun Land Trust (AMLT) is a Native-led, non-profit organization that serves as a vehicle for cultural relearning and the revitalization of Tribal connections to place through three core focal areas: Indigenous stewardship, conservation and restoration, and research and education.

Our ancestors recognized that the way we maintain balance in our life was by having healthy relationships with all living things and to ensure the sacredness of Mother Earth.

From defending sacred Tribal sites like Juristac, to preparing today's youth to be tomorrow's Tribal leaders, to restoring ceremony and sacredness to Popeloutchom (our ancestral lands), AMLT is working to support the Tribe's healing from the historical trauma of colonization and to support more just and sustainable environments and communities for all.

Three percent of the proceeds from sales of this book are donated to AMLT.

AmahMutsunLandTrust.org

About Our Nature Connection

Our Nature Connection inspires people to connect directly and mindfully with nature as a path to greater peace, joy, and healing in their lives and in the world.

We empower people to:
- Find simple ways to connect with the Earth in daily life,
- Cultivate intimate and nourishing bonds with wild places and more-than-human beings, and
- Access nature-based healing for mind, body, and spirit.

Our work is a gentle yet powerful integration of deep nature connection, mindfulness practice, and holistic healing—a unique approach we call *NatureWise.*

We offer a wealth of practices appropriate for diverse settings, and share them through group programs, individual sessions, consulting services, and the written word.

OurNatureConnection.com

Resources for Connecting with Nature

OurNatureConnection.com
Visit our website for more poems, practices, and information about our programs. Sign up to receive monthly infusions of nature-based goodness.

Turning Toward Nature
Learn how to deepen your connection with nature wherever you are through this four-week course, which features relaxing, restorative group calls and nourishing nature-based activities.

The Nature of Writing
Explore how nature inspires our writing, and how writing offers a powerful bridge to a deep and nourishing connection with nature through this six-week series, which includes live group calls and optional homework.

In-Person Nature Immersion Programs
Discover what it's like to connect more intimately and mindfully with the natural world, and what becomes possible when you do. Leave feeling relaxed and replenished, with simple tools you can use to connect with nature anytime, anywhere.

Individual Sessions
Face life's challenges with greater clarity and ease through skilled, personalized support. Learn how to receive healing and guidance from the natural world and activate your innate wisdom and creativity.

Consulting Services
Enliven and empower your professional work by tapping into nature's capacity to calm, heal, and inspire—outdoors, indoors, and even on Zoom! We can teach you simple yet potent practices to share with clients, help you design innovative group programs, or craft a custom program to meet your goals.

Learn more at OurNatureConnection.com

The book that started it all.

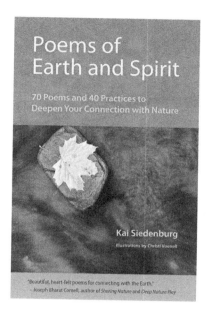

At turns peaceful, playful, and provocative, *Poems of Earth and Spirit* is a collection of poetry and practices that draws us into deeper kinship with all life. Through intimate original poems, we feel what it's like to walk on padded paws, to take wing, to root ourselves in the Earth. And through carefully crafted practices, we learn how to cultivate a direct connection with nature that supports and sustains us wherever we go.

"Beautiful, heart-felt poems for connecting with the Earth."

—Joseph Bharat Cornell, author of *Sharing Nature* and *Deep Nature Play*

2020 Next Generation Indie Book Awards Finalist

PoemsofEarthandSpirit.com

The journey continues. The voice deepens.
The terrain expands.

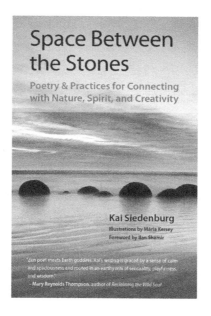

Beauty. Joy. Belonging. Our souls long for these things, and find them in this collection of poems and practices that call us home to our original bonds with nature, Spirit, and creativity. The poems surprise and delight, revealing a passionate love affair with nature and a friendly fluency with everyday spirituality. And the practices help us invite more authentic and nourishing connections into our own lives.

"Zen poet meets Earth Goddess. Kai's writing is graced by a sense of calm and spaciousness and rooted in an earthy mix of sensuality, playfulness, and wisdom."

—Mary Reynolds Thompson, author of *Reclaiming the Wild Soul*

2021 Next Generation Indie Book Awards Finalist

SpaceBetweentheStones.com